BEIJING TRAV.

Discover the Magic of the
Forbidden City: Your Ultimate
Beijing Adventure!

BY

Darrell L. Melton

Copyright

Table of Content

Personal Experience

As I ventured off the plane in Beijing, I was loaded up with fervour and expectation. This was my most memorable time in China, and I had heard such a great amount about the city's set of experiences, culture, and magnificence. I took a full breath and set myself up for the experience ahead.

My most memorable stop was the Prohibited City, a tremendous complex of royal residences, yards, and nurseries that had once been the supreme castle. As I strolled through the fabulous doors, I was struck by the greatness of the engineering and the tender loving care in each corner. It was not difficult to see the reason why this was quite possibly the main site in China's set of experiences.

Then, I visited the Incomparable Mass of China, perhaps the most notable milestone on the planet. I climbed along the wall, wondering about the stunning perspectives on the encompassing open country. As I strolled, I couldn't resist the opportunity to contemplate the large number of labourers who had fabricated this unbelievable construction quite a long time back.

My excursion to Beijing was unfinished without a visit to the Sanctuary of Paradise, an otherworldly haven settled in the core of the city. As I strolled through the tranquil nurseries, I felt a feeling of quiet and peacefulness that I had never experienced. Maybe the city's clamour and commotion had disappeared, leaving me in my very own universe.

I likewise visited Beihai Park, a quiet desert spring in the core of the city. The recreation area's delightful lakes, nurseries, and structures made it the ideal spot to get away from the clamour and disorder of the city. I went through hours meandering through the recreation area, absorbing the magnificence and peacefulness of my environmental factors.

One of the most critical encounters of my excursion was visiting Houhai Lake, a nightlife objective with a customary touch. As the sun set, the lights of the encompassing bars and cafés enlightened the lake, making an enchanted environment. I went through the night tasting tea and watching the boats float by, feeling like I was essential for a conventional Chinese canvas.

Thinking about my outing to Beijing, I was loaded up with recollections, examples, and motivation. I had found out such a huge amount about China's rich culture and history, and I had been moved by the glow and neighbourliness of the individuals I had met. As I gathered my packs and was ready to leave, I realize that I would convey these recollections with me until the end of my life.

As I loaded onto the plane back home, I felt a feeling of bitterness blended in with energy. While I was miserable leaving Beijing, I realize that there were still countless spots in China and the past that I needed to investigate. As the plane took off, I watched out at the city underneath and realize that I would be back again sometime in the not-so-distant future, prepared to proceed with my excursion through this mind-boggling country.

Introduction

Welcome to Beijing, the heart of China and a city that is rich in history, culture, and tradition. As one of the oldest and most populous cities in the world, Beijing is a must-see destination for anyone looking to experience the magic of China. From the majestic Forbidden City to the iconic Great Wall, there is no shortage of attractions to explore in this fascinating city.

Beijing, formerly known as Peking, is the capital city of China and has a history that dates back over 3,000 years. As the political, cultural, and educational centre of the country, it is a city that has played a pivotal role in shaping the history and culture of China. Today, Beijing is a modern metropolis that is home to over 21 million people and has become a major hub for international travel and commerce.

One of the most popular attractions in Beijing is the Forbidden City, which was once the imperial palace during the Ming and Qing dynasties. This magnificent palace complex covers an area of 720,000 square meters and is home to over 9,000 rooms. It is a true architectural wonder and a testament to the opulence and grandeur of imperial China. Visitors can explore the various halls, palaces, and courtyards within the Forbidden City and learn about the history and culture of China's emperors.

Another iconic attraction in Beijing is the Great Wall of China, which stretches over 13,000 miles across the country. The section of the wall that is closest to Beijing is the Badaling Great Wall, which is a popular destination for tourists. Visitors can hike along the wall and take in the breathtaking views of the surrounding mountains and countryside. The

Great Wall is a testament to the ingenuity and determination of the Chinese people, and it is a must-see attraction for anyone visiting Beijing.

In addition to its historical and cultural attractions, Beijing is also a city that is known for its modern architecture, vibrant nightlife, and delicious cuisine. The city has undergone a rapid transformation in recent years and is now home to some of the most innovative and cutting-edge buildings in the world. One such building is the Beijing National Stadium, also known as the Bird's Nest, which was built for the 2008 Summer Olympics. Visitors can take a tour of the stadium and learn about its unique design and construction.

When it comes to nightlife, Beijing has something for everyone. From trendy nightclubs and bars to traditional tea houses and live music venues, there is no shortage of entertainment options in the city. The

Houhai Lake area is a popular destination for nightlife, with its picturesque setting and numerous bars and restaurants.

No visit to Beijing would be complete without sampling the city's famous cuisine. Beijing cuisine is known for its bold flavours and use of local ingredients, such as Beijing duck, jiaozi (dumplings), and baozi (steamed buns). Visitors can try these and other local specialities at the city's many restaurants and food stalls.

Beyond its attractions, Beijing is a city that is steeped in tradition and culture. From the ancient practices of traditional Chinese medicine to the vibrant art scene and festivals that celebrate Chinese culture, there is always something new to discover in Beijing. Visitors can take a Hutong tour to explore the city's narrow alleyways and learn about the daily lives of Beijing's residents.

Beijing is a city that is rich in history, culture, and tradition, and it is a must-see destination for anyone looking to experience the magic of China. From the majestic Forbidden City to the iconic Great Wall, there is no shortage of attractions to explore in this fascinating city. Whether you are interested in history, culture, architecture, or cuisine, Beijing has something to offer everyone. So come and discover the magic of Beijing, and experience the the splendour attach to it

Population

Beijing, the capital city of the People's Republic of China, is one of the most populous cities in the world. With its rich cultural heritage, bustling streets, and towering skyscrapers, Beijing is home to millions of people, both locals and visitors alike. Understanding the population of Beijing is essential for anyone who plans to visit or live in the city.

As of 2021, the population of Beijing is estimated to be around 21 million people. The city has experienced significant population growth over the past few decades, and this growth shows no signs of slowing down. Beijing's population is a mix of both permanent residents and migrants who come to the city for work, education, or other opportunities.

In terms of gender distribution, Beijing has more males than females. According to the latest statistics, there are approximately 11 million males and 10 million females in the city. This is a significant difference, and it is attributed to various factors such as the one-child policy, which led to a preference for male children, and the traditional belief that males are better suited for certain jobs or roles.

Despite the gender imbalance, Beijing is a vibrant and diverse city that is home to people of different ages, cultures, and backgrounds. The city is divided into different districts, each with its unique characteristics and demographics. Some of the most populous districts include Chaoyang, Haidian, and Fengtai.

Chaoyang is the largest district in Beijing, with a population of over 3.6 million people. It is known for its commercial and business areas, including the Central Business District (CBD), which is home to many international companies and high-end shopping centres. Haidian, on the other hand, is home to some of China's top universities, including Peking University and Tsinghua University, as well as numerous tech companies, making it a popular destination for students and professionals.

Fengtai is a more residential district and is home to many migrant workers who come to Beijing in search of better job opportunities. It is also known for its parks, such as the popular World Park, which features miniature versions of famous landmarks from around the world.

In addition to the different districts, Beijing also has a significant ex-pat community, with people from all over the world living and working in the city. This diversity adds to the richness and complexity of the city and makes it an exciting place to explore and experience.

As with any city, understanding the population of Beijing is essential for anyone who plans to visit or live there. Knowing the demographics of the city can help you navigate its streets, understand its culture, and appreciate its unique characteristics. Whether you are a visitor or a resident, Beijing is a city that offers endless opportunities for adventure, exploration, and discovery.

Weather and Climate

Beijing, the capital city of China, has a humid continental climate, characterized by hot and humid summers and cold and dry winters. It experiences four distinct seasons, with each season offering unique experiences for visitors to the city.

Summer in Beijing starts in June and lasts until August. This season is characterized by high temperatures and humidity, with occasional thunderstorms. The average temperature during this season ranges from 25°C to 35°C (77°F to 95°F). It is advisable to carry light and breathable clothing to cope with the heat. Summer is also the peak tourist season, and visitors can expect crowds at popular attractions such as the Great Wall of China and the Forbidden City.

Autumn in Beijing starts in September and lasts until November. It is characterized by cool and dry weather, with clear skies and comfortable temperatures. The average temperature during this season ranges from 12°C to 22°C (54°F to 72°F). This is a great time to visit Beijing as the crowds have thinned out, and the foliage turns into vibrant shades of red and gold.

Winter in Beijing starts in December and lasts until February. It is characterized by cold and dry weather, with occasional snowfall. The average temperature during this season ranges from -10°C to 5°C (14°F to 41°F). Visitors should carry warm clothing such as jackets, sweaters, and boots to cope with the cold. Winter is also a great time to visit Beijing for those who love winter sports, as there are numerous ski resorts in the city.

Spring in Beijing starts in March and lasts until May. It is characterized by mild and pleasant weather, with occasional sandstorms from the Gobi Desert. The average temperature during this season ranges from 8°C to 20°C (46°F to 68°F). This is a great time to visit Beijing as the weather is comfortable, and the city comes alive with cherry blossoms.

In addition to the four distinct seasons, Beijing also experiences two rainy seasons, one in late summer and the other in early summer. The rainy season in late summer usually starts in July and lasts until August, while the rainy season in early summer usually starts in May and lasts until June. Visitors should carry umbrellas or raincoats during these seasons to avoid getting wet.

It is important to note that the climate in Beijing can be unpredictable, with occasional extreme weather conditions such as heatwaves, cold snaps, and sandstorms. Visitors should always check the weather forecast before travelling to Beijing and carry appropriate clothing to cope with the weather.

In conclusion, the weather and climate of Beijing are diverse, with each season offering unique experiences for visitors. It is important to plan ahead and carry appropriate clothing to cope with the weather, especially during extreme weather conditions. Regardless of the season, visitors can always find something to do in Beijing, from exploring the city's rich history and culture to indulging in its diverse culinary offerings.

Popular Sporting Activities

Beijing is a city that boasts a long and proud history of sports, dating back to ancient times. Today, it is home to a variety of popular sports, both traditional and modern, that attract locals and visitors alike.

Let's take a closer look at some of the most popular sporting activities in Beijing and the differences in participation between men and women.

One of the most popular sports in Beijing is basketball. The sport has gained immense popularity in recent years, with many Chinese players joining the NBA and helping to spread the game's popularity. Beijing has several basketball courts throughout the city, which are open to the public. The sport is played by both men and women, with men typically playing at a more competitive level than women.

Another popular sport in Beijing is badminton. The sport is played in parks, recreational centres, and clubs throughout the city, and it is widely enjoyed by both men and women. Badminton is considered a very important sport in China, and the country has produced some of the world's top players.

Football, also known as soccer in some parts of the world, is another sport that is growing in popularity in Beijing. The city has several professional football clubs, and the sport is also played by amateurs in parks and other recreational areas. Men typically dominate the sport at a competitive level, but women also enjoy playing the sport recreationally.

Table tennis is another sport that is widely enjoyed in Beijing, and China is considered to be the dominant country in the sport. The sport is played by both men and women, and many local parks have outdoor tables available for public use.

Martial arts are also a significant part of Beijing's sporting culture. Tai chi and other forms of traditional Chinese martial arts are practised by both men and women throughout the city. Many martial arts schools offer classes to people of all ages and skill levels, and it's not uncommon to see people practising in parks or other public spaces.

When it comes to differences in participation between men and women, it's important to note that traditional gender roles and expectations still play a significant role in Chinese society. This is particularly true when it comes to sports. While both men and women participate in many of the same sports in Beijing, men are generally more likely to participate in competitive sports and receive support from their families to pursue athletic careers. Women, on the other hand, may face more barriers to participating in sports at a competitive level, particularly if they come from more traditional families.

Despite these challenges, many women in Beijing are breaking down barriers and making their mark in the world of sports. Women's football, for example, has seen a surge in popularity in recent years, and more women are pursuing careers as professional athletes. In addition, many grassroots organizations are working to promote gender equality in sports and to provide opportunities for women to participate at all levels.

In conclusion, Beijing offers a wide range of sporting activities for both men and women, from traditional martial arts to modern team sports. While gender roles and expectations may still play a role in determining who participates in certain sports at a competitive level, the city is making strides towards promoting gender equality in sports and providing opportunities for all to participate and enjoy. Whether you're a seasoned athlete or just looking to try something new, Beijing's vibrant sporting culture has something for everyone.

Official Languages

Beijing, the capital city of China is home to a diverse group of people with various ethnic and linguistic backgrounds. The official language in Beijing, and across China, is Mandarin Chinese, which is also known as Standard Chinese or Putonghua. However, in addition to Mandarin, there are several other dialects and minority languages spoken in the city.

In Beijing, most people speak Mandarin Chinese, which is a tonal language with four basic tones plus a neutral tone. Mandarin Chinese is the most widely spoken language in the world, with over 1 billion speakers globally. As the official language of the People's Republic of China, it is the language of government, education, and business.

In addition to Mandarin Chinese, there are several other dialects spoken in Beijing, including the

Beijing dialect, which is also known as Beijing Mandarin or Pekingese. This dialect is a variant of Mandarin and has some distinct differences in pronunciation, vocabulary, and grammar compared to standard Mandarin.

Apart from Mandarin and its dialects, other minority languages are spoken in Beijing. These include Mongolian, Tibetan, Uyghur, and Korean, among others. While these languages are not as widely spoken as Mandarin, they play a significant role in Beijing's cultural diversity and heritage.

The Mongolian language, for example, is spoken by the Mongolian minority population in Beijing. The Mongolian ethnic group has a long history in China and has influenced Chinese culture in various ways, including language, religion, and cuisine. Tibetan is also spoken by the Tibetan minority population in Beijing. The Tibetan people have a unique culture, and their language is closely related to the Burmese and Himalayan languages.

Uyghur is another minority language spoken in Beijing, mainly by the Uyghur ethnic group, who have their roots in the Xinjiang region in western China. Uyghur is a Turkic language and has some similarities with Turkish and Uzbek.

Apart from the minority languages, English is also widely spoken in Beijing, especially in the central business district, tourist areas, and by younger generations. However, the level of English proficiency varies among the population, with some being fluent in the language while others only speak a few basic phrases.

In conclusion, Beijing is a linguistically diverse city with Mandarin Chinese as the official language and several other dialects and minority languages spoken by different ethnic groups. The city's linguistic diversity is a reflection of China's rich cultural heritage and contributes to its unique identity.

Chapter1: Welcome to Beijing; the Heart of China

Welcome to Beijing, the vibrant and bustling capital city of China. Known as the heart of the country, Beijing is a city that is steeped in history, culture, and tradition, and it is a must-visit destination for anyone looking to experience the magic of China.

With a population of over 21 million people, Beijing is a city that is constantly in motion. From the rush of morning commuters to the lively bustle of the city's many markets and shops, there is always something happening in Beijing. Despite its fast pace, the city remains deeply connected to its rich cultural heritage, and visitors to Beijing can experience this unique blend of old and new at every turn.

One of the most iconic attractions in Beijing is the Forbidden City, which was once the imperial palace of China's emperors. This sprawling complex covers over 180 acres and contains over 9000 rooms, making it one of the largest palace complexes in the world. As you explore the Forbidden City, you'll be transported back in time to the days of the Ming and Qing dynasties, and you'll marvel at the opulence and grandeur of this ancient palace.

Another must-visit attraction in Beijing is the Great Wall of China. Stretching over 13,000 miles, the Great Wall is a testament to the ingenuity and perseverance of the Chinese people. Visitors to Beijing can hike along the Great Wall, taking in breathtaking views of the surrounding mountains and countryside. As you walk along this ancient wonder, you'll feel a deep sense of awe and wonder, and you'll gain a newfound appreciation for the incredible achievements of the people who built it.

Beyond its historical attractions, Beijing is a city that is bursting with energy and vitality. From the colourful markets and street vendors of the city's many neighbourhoods to the trendy bars and clubs of the Sanlitun area, there is always something exciting to see and do in Beijing. Whether you're looking for a relaxing afternoon in a traditional tea house or an exhilarating night out on the town, you'll find it all in this dynamic city.

Of course, no visit to Beijing would be complete without sampling the city's famous cuisine. Beijing cuisine is known for its bold flavours and creative use of local ingredients, and visitors to the city can indulge in a wide range of delicious dishes. From the succulent Peking duck to the savoury jiaozi dumplings, Beijing's cuisine is a feast for the senses. You can also explore the city's many food markets and street vendors, where you'll find an endless array of snacks and treats to savour.

But perhaps the most memorable aspect of a visit to Beijing is the warmth and hospitality of its people. Beijing residents are friendly, welcoming, and always eager to share their culture and traditions with visitors. Whether you're taking a stroll through a local park or exploring the city's many historical landmarks, you'll encounter locals who are eager to share their stories and experiences with you.

In conclusion, Beijing is a city that is bursting with life and energy, and it offers visitors an incredible glimpse into the rich cultural heritage of China. From the majestic Forbidden City to the awe-inspiring Great Wall, Beijing is a city that will leave you breathless and awestruck. But it's not just the historical attractions that make Beijing so special. It's also the people, the food, and the unique blend of old and new that make this city such an enchanting destination. So come and experience the magic of Beijing for yourself, and discover why this city truly is the heart of China.

Why Beijing Should Be Your Next Travel Destination

If you're looking for a travel destination that combines ancient history with modern innovation, then look no further than Beijing, the capital city of China. With a rich cultural heritage, world-famous landmarks, and a vibrant modern atmosphere, Beijing has everything you need for an unforgettable travel experience. In this article, we'll take a closer look at why Beijing should be your next travel destination.

First and foremost, Beijing is home to some of the most iconic landmarks in the world. The Great Wall of China, one of the Seven Wonders of the World, stretches over 13,000 miles across the country, and the most famous section of it is located just outside of Beijing. Hiking along the Great Wall is a once-in-a-lifetime experience, as you take in breathtaking views of the surrounding mountains and countryside.

Another must-see attraction in Beijing is the Forbidden City, an enormous complex of palaces and courtyards that was once the home of Chinese emperors. The Forbidden City is a UNESCO World Heritage Site, and visitors can explore its many buildings, halls, and gardens to gain a deeper understanding of China's imperial past.

But Beijing isn't just about history and tradition - it's also a modern, bustling metropolis that offers visitors a glimpse into China's contemporary culture. The city's thriving arts scene is evident in its many museums, galleries, and theatres, where you can experience traditional Chinese art forms like calligraphy, painting, and opera, as well as modern art exhibitions and performances.

Beijing is also a city of contrasts, with traditional markets and street vendors selling local delicacies like Peking duck and jiaozi dumplings, alongside trendy bars and restaurants serving up innovative fusion cuisine.

One of the most striking things about Beijing is its sheer size and scale. With a population of over 21 million people, Beijing is one of the most populous cities in the world, and it offers endless opportunities for exploration and discovery. Visitors can get lost in the narrow hutong alleys of the city's traditional neighbourhoods, where locals go about their daily lives, or they can explore the modern skyscrapers and shopping malls of the central business district.

Whatever your interests, there's something for everyone in Beijing. Another reason to visit Beijing is the warmth and hospitality of its people. Despite its size and fast pace, Beijing is a city that is deeply connected to its cultural heritage, and locals are always eager to share their traditions and customs with visitors. Whether you're practising tai chi in a local park or chatting with a street vendor over a steaming bowl of noodles, you'll encounter friendly and welcoming locals who are proud of their city and eager to show it off.

Finally, Beijing is a city that is constantly evolving and changing. With new construction projects and developments underway, there's always something new to discover in Beijing. The city will be hosting the Winter Olympics in 2022, which means that visitors will have the opportunity to experience world-class sporting events and cultural performances. This event is sure to put Beijing even more firmly on the global stage, and it's the perfect time to plan your visit to this incredible city.

In conclusion, Beijing is a travel destination that offers something for everyone. Whether you're a history buff, a foodie, an art lover, or simply looking to experience the unique energy and atmosphere of a dynamic city, Beijing is a perfect choice. From its iconic landmarks and cultural heritage to its modern innovations and warm hospitality, Beijing is a city that will leave you spellbound and inspired. So why not make Beijing your next travel destination and experience the magic for yourself?

How to Use This Guidebook

Welcome to the Beijing Travel Guide 2023! This book is designed to help you make the most of your visit to the capital city of China, providing you with insider tips, practical advice, and detailed information about everything from must-see attractions to hidden gems. In this section, we'll guide you through how to use this book to plan your perfect trip to Beijing.

The first thing you should do is take a look at the table of contents, which lists all the chapters and sections in the book. This will help you get an overview of the information available, so you can plan your reading and focus on the areas that interest you most. The table of contents is divided into six main sections:

Introduction: This section provides a general overview of Beijing, including its history, culture, and geography. It's a great place to start if you're new to the city or want to learn more about its background.

Welcome to Beijing: The Heart of China: This chapter explores what makes Beijing such a unique and fascinating travel destination, with a focus on its famous landmarks, cultural heritage, and modern innovations.

Why Beijing Should Be Your Next Travel Destination: This section provides a more detailed look at the top reasons to visit Beijing, from its iconic landmarks and vibrant arts scene to its warm hospitality and constant evolution.

Planning Your Trip to Beijing: This chapter offers practical advice on how to plan your trip, including information on visas, flights, accommodations, and transportation. It also includes tips on when to visit, what to pack, and how to stay safe and healthy while travelling.

Exploring Beijing: This section is the heart of the guide, offering detailed information on all the must-see attractions, hidden gems, and local experiences in Beijing. It's divided into several chapters, each focusing on a different area of the city, such as the Forbidden City, the Great Wall, and the Hutongs.

Getting Around Beijing: This chapter provides information on the best ways to get around the city, including public transportation, taxis, and bicycles. It also includes tips on navigating the language barrier and getting help in case of emergencies.

Once you've familiarized yourself with the contents of the book, you can start exploring each section in more detail. Each chapter is designed to be read independently, so you can skip around and focus on the areas that interest you most. Each section includes practical tips, insider advice, and detailed information on everything from admission fees to opening hours, so you can plan your itinerary with confidence.

Throughout the book, you'll also find helpful features like maps, photos, and special tips called "Insider Knowledge," which provide valuable insights from local experts. These features are designed to help you make the most of your trip and discover the best of what Beijing has to offer.

Finally, don't forget to use the index at the back of the book, which provides a quick reference guide to all the key topics and locations mentioned in the guide. This will help you find the information you need quickly and easily, no matter where you are in the book.

The Beijing Travel Guide 2023 is a comprehensive and user-friendly guidebook that will help you plan your perfect trip to one of the world's most fascinating cities. By following the tips and advice in this book, you'll be able to explore the best of Beijing's history, culture, and modern innovations, and have an unforgettable travel experience. So, let's get started!

Chapter 2: Getting Ready for Your Trip

Best Time to Visit Beijing

Beijing, the capital of China, is an incredible city that attracts millions of tourists every year. But when is the best time to visit Beijing? This question can be a bit tricky to answer because the city experiences four distinct seasons with varying temperatures and weather patterns. However, in this section, we'll guide you through the factors that can influence your decision and help you find the perfect time to visit Beijing.

Spring (March to May)

Spring is one of the most popular times to visit Beijing because the weather is mild and comfortable. The temperatures are usually between 10°C to 20°C, and the city is surrounded by beautiful cherry blossoms and other flowers that

44

create a stunning atmosphere. During this season, you can visit some of Beijing's most famous landmarks, such as the Forbidden City and the Great Wall, without the crowds of summer. However, keep in mind that the weather can be unpredictable, and there can be occasional sandstorms in the spring.

Summer (June to August)

Summer is the peak tourist season in Beijing because the weather is hot and sunny, making it a great time to explore the city's outdoor attractions. The average temperature during this season is around 25°C to 30°C, and the days are long, giving you more time to explore. However, the downside of visiting during summer is that the city can be crowded, and the humidity can be intense, making it uncomfortable to spend extended periods outside. It's also worth noting that this is the rainy season, so you may experience occasional thunderstorms.

Autumn (September to November)

Autumn is another great time to visit Beijing because the weather is mild, and the city is filled with colourful autumn foliage. The temperature during this season is around 10°C to 20°C, making it ideal for outdoor activities like hiking and sightseeing. This is also a great time to taste Beijing's delicious food, such as roasted chestnuts and hot pot. However, like spring, the weather can be unpredictable, and it can get quite chilly towards the end of autumn.

Winter (December to February)

Winter is the low season for tourism in Beijing because the temperatures are often below freezing, and there is a chance of snow. However, it can be a magical time to visit the city, especially during the Lunar New Year festivities, when the streets are filled with colourful lanterns, and there are many cultural performances to enjoy. The upside of visiting during winter is that the city is less crowded, and you can enjoy attractions like the Forbidden City and the Great Wall without the crowds of other seasons. Additionally, winter sports like skiing and snowboarding are popular activities in the nearby mountains.

So, when should you go to Beijing? Ultimately, the best time to visit depends on your preferences and interests. If you don't like crowds, you might want to avoid the summer season. However, if you're a fan of warm weather and outdoor activities, summer might be the perfect time for you. If you're looking for a more comfortable temperature and beautiful scenery, spring and autumn are great options. And if you want to experience the festive spirit of Beijing's winter season, December to February could be the perfect time for you.

On these above, Beijing is a city that can be enjoyed year-round, with each season offering something unique and special. By considering the weather, crowds, and seasonal events, you can plan your trip to Beijing at the best time for you. Whatever time of year you choose to visit, you're sure to have an unforgettable experience in one of the world's most fascinating cities.

Top Attractions In Beijing

Beijing is a city that's steeped in history and culture, with an incredible array of attractions to explore. From ancient landmarks to modern marvels, Beijing has something for everyone. In this section, we'll take a look at some of the top attractions that you shouldn't miss when visiting Beijing.

The Great Wall of China

One of the most famous landmarks in the world, the Great Wall of China is an iconic sight that stretches for thousands of kilometres through northern China. The Great Wall is an impressive feat of engineering that was built over 2,000 years ago to protect the Chinese empire from invasion. Today, you can hike along the wall and take in the breathtaking views of the surrounding landscape.

The Forbidden City

Located in the heart of Beijing, the Forbidden City is a UNESCO World Heritage Site that was the former imperial palace of the Ming and Qing dynasties. This sprawling complex consists of over 980 buildings, and it's one of the best-preserved examples of ancient Chinese architecture. Visitors can explore the various palaces, halls, and gardens within the complex, which provide a glimpse into the opulent lifestyle of China's emperors.

Temple of Heaven

The Temple of Heaven is a magnificent temple complex that was built during the Ming dynasty. It was used by emperors to pray for good harvests and to perform sacrificial ceremonies. The temple is surrounded by beautiful gardens and is a peaceful oasis in the heart of the city. Visitors can explore the various halls and pavilions within the complex and witness traditional Chinese music and dance performances.

Summer Palace

The Summer Palace is a vast imperial garden that was once the summer retreat of the Qing dynasty emperors. This stunning complex is set around a lake and is filled with beautiful gardens, pavilions, and temples. Visitors can explore the various buildings within the complex, take a boat ride on the lake, or simply relax and enjoy the serene surroundings.

Tiananmen Square

Tiananmen Square is one of the largest public squares in the world and is located in the heart of Beijing. This historic square has been the site of many important events in Chinese history, including the proclamation of the People's Republic of China in 1949. Visitors can take in the impressive architecture of the surrounding buildings, including the Monument to the People's Heroes and the Mao Zedong Memorial Hall.

The Lama Temple

The Lama Temple is a beautiful Buddhist temple that was built during the Qing dynasty. It's one of the largest and most important Tibetan Buddhist temples outside of Tibet, and it's filled with stunning works of art and architecture. Visitors can explore the various halls and pavilions within the temple complex and witness traditional Tibetan Buddhist ceremonies.

Beijing National Stadium

The Beijing National Stadium, also known as the Bird's Nest, is a stunning piece of modern architecture that was built for the 2008 Olympic Games. The stadium is an impressive sight, with its unique steel framework and bird's nest shape. Visitors can take a guided tour of the stadium and learn about its history and design.

Beijing is a city that's filled with incredible attractions that offer a glimpse into China's rich history and culture. From ancient landmarks to modern marvels, there's something for everyone to explore and discover in Beijing. Whether you're interested in exploring ancient palaces and temples, hiking along the Great Wall, or marvelling at modern architecture, Beijing has it all. So, pack your bags and get ready to explore one of the world's most fascinating cities.

How to Get to Beijing

Beijing is one of the most popular travel destinations in the world, with millions of visitors arriving each year from all corners of the globe. If you're planning a trip to Beijing, you'll need to consider the best ways to get there. In this section, we'll take a look at the various transportation options available, including flights, trains, and local transportation.

Flights

Beijing is served by two main airports: Beijing Capital International Airport and Beijing Daxing International Airport. Beijing Capital International Airport is one of the busiest airports in the world, with flights arriving from all major cities around the globe. It's located 26 kilometres northeast of the city centre and is easily accessible by taxi, subway, and shuttle bus.

Beijing Daxing International Airport is a newer airport that opened in 2019 and is located 46 kilometres south of the city centre. It's currently served by several international airlines, including British Airways, Finnair, and LOT Polish Airlines. Like Beijing Capital International Airport, it's accessible by taxi, subway, and shuttle bus.

When booking flights to Beijing, it's important to check for deals and promotions offered by airlines. It's also recommended to book flights well in advance to secure the best prices.

Trains

If you're travelling to Beijing from within China, taking a train is a convenient and affordable option. Beijing has four main railway stations: Beijing Railway Station, Beijing West Railway Station, Beijing South Railway Station, and Beijing North Railway Station.

Beijing Railway Station is the oldest and largest railway station in Beijing, and it's located in the city centre. It's the main hub for trains travelling to and from northern China.

Beijing West Railway Station is one of the busiest railway stations in Asia, serving high-speed trains to destinations throughout China, including Shanghai, Xi'an, and Guangzhou.

Beijing South Railway Station is the largest high-speed railway station in Asia and is the hub for trains travelling to and from southern China.

Beijing North Railway Station serves trains to and from the northern provinces of China, including Inner Mongolia and Hebei.

Local Transportation

Once you've arrived in Beijing, there are several options for local transportation, including taxis, subways, buses, and bike sharing.

Taxis are readily available in Beijing and are a convenient way to get around the city. However, be sure to only use licensed taxis and to negotiate the fare before getting in.

The Beijing Subway is one of the most convenient and affordable ways to get around the city. It's clean, safe, and easy to use, with signs and announcements in both Chinese and English.

Buses are also a convenient way to get around Beijing, with routes covering most of the city. However, be prepared for crowded buses and long wait times during peak hours.

Finally, bike sharing has become increasingly popular in Beijing, with several companies offering bike rental services throughout the city. It's a great way to explore the city at your own pace and to avoid traffic congestion.

Getting to Beijing and navigating the city's transportation options is relatively straightforward. Whether you're arriving by plane, train, or bus, there are several options available to suit your needs and budget. Once in Beijing, the subway, buses, taxis, and bike sharing are all convenient ways to get around and explore the city. With a little planning and research, you can easily make the most of your time in this fascinating and vibrant city.

Different departure Times at Trains and Bus Stations

Beijing, the capital city of China, is a bustling metropolis that attracts millions of tourists every year. One of the best ways to explore the city is by taking a train or bus, which offers a unique opportunity to see the city's sights and sounds from a different perspective. When planning your trip to Beijing, it is essential to know the different departure times for trains and buses to ensure you make the most of your time in the city.

Trains in Beijing are an efficient and affordable way to travel around the city and its outskirts. The city has several railway stations, each serving different regions of the country. The most popular station is the Beijing Railway Station, which is located in the heart of the city and serves as a major hub for both long-distance and local trains. The station operates trains to most of the major cities in China, including Shanghai, Guangzhou, and Xi'an.

Train schedules in Beijing vary depending on the season, the day of the week, and the route you intend to take. The most common train departure times in Beijing are early in the morning or late at night. However, some trains may depart in the afternoon or evening, depending on the destination. It is recommended to book your train tickets in advance, especially during peak travel seasons like the Chinese New Year or National Day Holiday.

Buses are another popular mode of transportation in Beijing, offering a convenient and affordable way to travel around the city. The city has several bus terminals, including the Dongzhimen Bus Terminal, which is located in the central business district and serves as a hub for long-distance buses. The other major bus terminals in the city include the Beijing West Bus Station and the Beijing South Bus Station.

The bus schedules in Beijing vary depending on the route, time of day, and the terminal you depart from. Generally, buses in Beijing start running early in the morning and operate until late at night. However, some routes may only operate during specific hours of the day. It is essential to plan your trip and check the schedules in advance, especially if you intend to take a long-distance bus.

When planning your trip to Beijing, it is also important to consider the time it takes to travel to your destination. Depending on the route, trains and buses in Beijing can take anywhere from a few hours to several days. It is recommended to choose a comfortable and convenient mode of transportation that suits your travel needs and budget.

Beijing offers a variety of transportation options to help you explore the city and beyond. Whether you prefer to take the train or bus, it is essential to know the different departure times and schedules to ensure a hassle-free journey. With a little bit of planning and preparation, you can make the most of your time in this vibrant city and create unforgettable memories that will last a lifetime.

Visa Requirements and Other Travel Tips

If you're planning a trip to Beijing, one of the most important things to consider is the visa requirements. In this section, we'll take a look at the visa requirements for travelling to Beijing, as well as some other important travel tips to help make your trip as smooth and enjoyable as possible.

Visa Requirements

If you're travelling to Beijing from most countries, you'll need to apply for a Chinese visa before you arrive. The process can take several weeks, so it's important to start the application process well in advance of your trip. You can apply for a Chinese visa at your local Chinese embassy or consulate.

There are several types of Chinese visas available, including tourist visas, business visas, and student visas. If you're travelling to Beijing as a tourist, you'll need to apply for a tourist visa. Tourist visas are usually valid for 30 to 90 days, depending on your nationality and the purpose of your visit.

To apply for a Chinese tourist visa, you'll need to provide several documents, including a passport with at least six months of validity remaining, a completed visa application form, and a recent passport-sized photo. You'll also need to provide evidence of your travel arrangements, such as flight and hotel bookings, and proof of sufficient funds to cover your stay in Beijing.

Other Travel Tips

In addition to visa requirements, there are several other important travel tips to keep in mind when visiting Beijing.

Language: Mandarin Chinese is the official language of China, and while many people in Beijing speak some English, it's still a good idea to learn some basic Mandarin phrases to help you get around and communicate with locals.

Currency: The currency in Beijing is the Chinese Yuan (CNY). You can exchange foreign currency at banks, exchange booths, and hotels. It's also recommended to bring a credit card that's accepted in China, such as Visa or Mastercard.

Safety: Beijing is generally a safe city for travellers, but it's still important to take precautions to ensure your safety. Be aware of your surroundings, especially in crowded areas like tourist attractions and public transport. Avoid carrying large amounts of cash or valuable items, and be cautious when using ATMs.

Weather: Beijing experiences four distinct seasons, with hot summers and cold winters. The best time to visit Beijing is in the spring or fall when temperatures are mild and the weather is pleasant. Be sure to pack appropriate clothing for the season, including warm layers in the winter and light clothing in the summer.

Culture: Beijing has a rich cultural heritage, and it's important to respect local customs and traditions. When visiting temples and other religious sites, dress modestly and remove your shoes before entering. It's also important to be respectful of local customs and practices, such as not taking photos of people without their permission.

Travelling to Beijing requires careful planning and preparation, including obtaining the necessary visa and understanding local customs and traditions. By following these tips and taking the time to research and plan your trip, you can ensure a smooth and enjoyable visit to this fascinating and vibrant city.

Chapter 3: Exploring Beijing's Top Attractions

Unravelling the Secrets of the Imperial Palace

The Forbidden City is one of Beijing's most iconic landmarks and for good reason. This magnificent imperial palace was once the residence of China's emperors, and its sprawling complex of buildings and courtyards are filled with fascinating history and culture. In this section, we'll explore the secrets of the Forbidden City and uncover its rich and complex history.

History of the Forbidden City

The Forbidden City was built during the Ming Dynasty (1368-1644) and served as the imperial palace for more than 500 years. It was home to 24 emperors of the Ming and Qing Dynasties, and its construction involved more than a million workers and craftsmen. The palace complex is made up of nearly 1,000 buildings and covers an area of 180 acres, making it one of the largest palace complexes in the world.

The Forbidden City was designed to be the centre of the universe, with its north-south axis aligned with the traditional cosmological concept of the universe. It was surrounded by a moat and a 10-meter-high wall, which were designed to keep out intruders and protect the imperial family from attacks.

The palace was called the "Forbidden City" because it was strictly off-limits to anyone who wasn't a member of the imperial family or their closest advisors. Commoners were not allowed to enter the palace without special permission, and even high-ranking officials were only allowed to enter certain parts of the palace.

The architecture of the Forbidden City
The architecture of the Forbidden City is a stunning example of traditional Chinese palace design. The complex is made up of a series of courtyards and buildings, each with its unique features and purposes. The buildings are constructed from wood and feature elaborate decorations and carvings.

The most famous buildings in the Forbidden City are the Hall of Supreme Harmony, the Hall of Central Harmony, and the Hall of Preserving Harmony. These three buildings are located on the central axis of the palace and were used for important ceremonies and events. The Hall of Supreme Harmony is the largest and most important building in the palace and was used for imperial coronations and other important ceremonies.

Other notable buildings in the palace complex include the Palace of Heavenly Purity, the Palace of Earthly Tranquility, and the Imperial Garden. The Palace of Heavenly Purity was the residence of the emperors and was also used for important imperial ceremonies. The Imperial Garden was a private garden for the imperial family and features beautiful landscaping and traditional Chinese architecture.

Uncovering the Secrets of the Forbidden City

Despite its long history and prominence in Chinese culture, the Forbidden City still holds many secrets waiting to be uncovered. One of the most fascinating aspects of the palace is its collection of artefacts and treasures, which include everything from ancient scrolls to priceless works of art.

Another interesting feature of the Forbidden City is its network of underground tunnels, which were used by the imperial family to travel between different parts of the palace. These tunnels are still being explored and studied by historians and archaeologists, and they offer a glimpse into the daily lives of the emperors and their families.

Visiting the Forbidden City

If you're planning a trip to Beijing, a visit to the Forbidden City is a must-see attraction. To make the most of your visit, be sure to plan and purchase your tickets in advance. You should also wear comfortable shoes and clothing, as the palace complex is quite large and requires a fair amount of walking.

While exploring the palace, be sure to take in the intricate details of the architecture and decorations. You can also learn more about the history of the palace by visiting the on-site museum and taking a guided tour.

Of course, the Forbidden City is a fascinating and iconic attraction in Beijing, filled with history, culture, and secrets waiting to be explored.

The Great Wall of China

The Great Wall of China is one of the world's most iconic and recognizable landmarks and for good reason. Stretching over 13,000 miles, it is one of the longest walls in the world and a testament to the ingenuity and perseverance of the Chinese people.

The wall was first built over 2,000 years ago, during the reign of the first Emperor of China, Qin Shi Huang. It was initially built as a means of protecting China's northern borders from invading nomadic tribes, and over the centuries it was continually expanded and reinforced by successive dynasties.

Today, visitors can explore the Great Wall at some different locations, each offering a unique perspective on this incredible feat of engineering.

One of the most popular sections of the wall is located at Badaling, just outside of Beijing. Here, visitors can walk along a well-preserved section of the wall, complete with watchtowers and ramparts, and take in the breathtaking views of the surrounding mountains and valleys.

Another popular destination is the Mutianyu section of the wall, which is located about an hour's drive from Beijing. This section is known for its stunning scenery, including forested hills and rugged terrain, as well as its well-preserved watchtowers and fortifications.

For those looking for a more adventurous experience, the Jinshanling section of the wall offers a challenging hike through some of the wall's most rugged and remote terrain. This section is less crowded than some of the more popular destinations and offers stunning views of the surrounding countryside.

Regardless of which section of the Great Wall you choose to explore, there is no denying the incredible history and culture that is embodied by this remarkable landmark. As you walk along the wall, you can't help but feel a sense of awe and wonder at the ingenuity and perseverance of the Chinese people who built it, and the sheer scale and magnitude of this engineering feat.

Visiting the Great Wall of China is truly an unforgettable experience and one that should be at the top of any traveller's bucket list. So why not plan your trip today and embark on a journey through time and history on one of the world's most iconic landmarks?

Temple of Heaven: A Spiritual Haven in the Heart of Beijing

The Temple of Heaven, located in the heart of Beijing, is one of the most stunning and unique architectural wonders in the world. It is a place of great historical and cultural significance, where emperors of the Ming and Qing dynasties would come to perform important rituals and offerings to the gods.

The temple complex is divided into three main sections: the Hall of Prayer for Good Harvests, the Imperial Vault of Heaven, and the Circular Mound Altar. Each of these sections served a specific purpose in the emperor's religious ceremonies, and are all equally impressive in their own right.

The Hall of Prayer for Good Harvests is the centrepiece of the temple complex and is one of the most striking examples of traditional Chinese architecture. It is a circular structure, with three tiers of eaves and a blue-tiled roof that is supported by 28 wooden pillars. The interior of the hall is just as impressive, with intricate carvings and paintings that depict the emperor's prayers for a bountiful harvest.

The Imperial Vault of Heaven is another impressive structure within the temple complex. It is a circular building with a conical roof and was used by the emperor to store the tablets of the gods. The interior of the vault is decorated with colourful paintings and intricate carvings, all of which are meant to symbolize the emperor's connection to the divine.

The Circular Mound Altar is the final section of the temple complex and is perhaps the most unique. It is a circular platform made of white marble and is surrounded by three concentric circles of stones. The altar was used by the emperor to perform important sacrifices and offerings to the gods and is said to represent the connection between heaven and earth.

While the Temple of Heaven is undoubtedly a stunning example of traditional Chinese architecture and design, it is also a place of great spiritual significance. For centuries, emperors and common people alike would come to the temple to pray for good fortune and blessings from the gods.

Today, visitors to the Temple of Heaven can experience the same sense of peace and tranquillity that generations before them have felt. The temple grounds are expansive and serene, with beautiful gardens and pavilions that are perfect for quiet reflection and contemplation.

Whether you are a history buff, a spiritual seeker, or simply someone who appreciates beautiful architecture and design, the Temple of Heaven is a must-see destination in Beijing. So why not plan your visit today and experience the wonder and beauty of this incredible cultural landmark for yourself?

Summer Palace: An Imperial Retreats of Garned and Lakes

The Summer Palace, located just outside of Beijing, is a magnificent complex of gardens, lakes, and palaces that served as the imperial retreat for the emperors of the Qing dynasty. It is one of the most impressive examples of traditional Chinese garden design and is a must-see destination for anyone visiting Beijing.

The Summer Palace was first constructed in the 12th century, but it was not until the Qing dynasty that it became the elaborate complex that we see today. The emperors of the Qing dynasty used the palace as a retreat from the pressures of court life in Beijing, and it quickly became one of the most beautiful and peaceful places in the empire.

The palace complex is centred around the stunning Kunming Lake, which covers an area of over 2.2 square kilometres. The lake is surrounded by rolling hills, pavilions, and gardens, and is a popular spot for boating and picnicking.

One of the most impressive features of the Summer Palace is the Longevity Hill, which rises over the lake and is home to several beautiful palaces and temples. The hill is adorned with pavilions and towers and offers breathtaking views of the surrounding gardens and lake.

The palace complex is also home to several other impressive structures, including the Hall of Benevolence and Longevity, the Hall of Joyful Longevity, and the Tower of Buddhist Incense. Each of these structures is decorated with intricate carvings and paintings and offers a unique glimpse into the art and culture of the Qing dynasty.

Perhaps the most impressive aspect of the Summer Palace, however, is the sheer beauty of the gardens and landscape. The palace grounds are home to countless species of plants and flowers, as well as a variety of wildlife, including birds, fish, and turtles. Visitors can spend hours wandering through the gardens, admiring the architecture and soaking up the peaceful atmosphere.

The Summer Palace is a true treasure of Chinese culture and history and is a must-see destination for anyone visiting Beijing. Whether you are a history buff, a nature lover, or simply someone who appreciates beautiful architecture and design, the Summer Palace is sure to leave you feeling inspired and amazed. So why not plan your visit today, and experience the wonder and beauty of this incredible imperial retreat for yourself?

The Symbol of China's Revolutionary Spirit

Tiananmen Square is perhaps one of the most iconic landmarks in China. Located in the heart of Beijing, it is a symbol of the country's revolutionary spirit and a place of immense historical significance.

The square is named after the Tiananmen Gate, which stands at the north end of the square and was once the main entrance to the Forbidden City. Today, the square covers an area of 109 acres and is surrounded by some important buildings, including the Great Hall of the People, the National Museum of China, and the Monument to the People's Heroes.

Tiananmen Square has played a pivotal role in China's history, serving as the site of many important events and demonstrations. Perhaps the most famous of these was the student-led protests that took place in 1989, which eventually culminated in the tragic Tiananmen Square Massacre.

Despite its troubled history, Tiananmen Square remains a symbol of the revolutionary spirit that has defined China for centuries. Visitors to the square can marvel at the sheer scale and grandeur of the space, as well as the many impressive monuments and structures that dot the landscape.

One of the most striking features of the square is the Monument to the People's Heroes, which stands at the centre of the square and serves as a tribute to those who lost their lives in the struggle for Chinese independence and freedom. The monument is flanked by two large marble pillars, which are engraved with images of key figures from Chinese history.

Another important structure in the square is the Great Hall of the People, which is home to the National People's Congress and serves as one of the most important political and cultural centres in China. The building is an impressive example of modern Chinese architecture, with its striking red and gold facade and grand interior spaces.

Visitors to Tiananmen Square can also take a stroll through the nearby National Museum of China, which offers a fascinating glimpse into the history and culture of this ancient civilization. The museum's extensive collection includes artefacts from all periods of Chinese history, from the prehistoric era to the present day.

No visit to Tiananmen Square would be complete without a visit to the Forbidden City, which lies just beyond the north gate. This ancient palace complex served as the residence of the Ming and Qing emperors for more than 500 years and is now a UNESCO World Heritage Site and one of China's most popular tourist attractions.

In conclusion, Tiananmen Square is a must-see destination for anyone visiting Beijing. Its rich history, iconic landmarks, and powerful symbolism make it a true symbol of China's revolutionary spirit and a testament to the country's enduring culture and heritage. So why not plan your visit today and experience the awe-inspiring beauty and history of this incredible landmark for yourself?

Beijing National Stadium

Beijing National Stadium, commonly known as the Bird's Nest, is one of the most recognizable structures in the world. The stadium, which was built for the 2008 Summer Olympics, is a marvel of modern architectural design, and its unique shape and intricate latticework have made it an icon of contemporary design.

The stadium was designed by the Swiss architects Jacques Herzog and Pierre de Meuron, and it was built by the Chinese construction company CITIC Construction. The construction of the stadium took over four years, and it cost an estimated $428 million.

The design of the stadium was inspired by Chinese ceramics and its intricate lattice structure was modelled after the woven baskets that are commonly used in Chinese craftwork. The stadium is made up of a series of interlocking steel beams, which give it its distinctive shape and also serve to provide support for the roof.

One of the most impressive features of the Bird's Nest is its roof, which is made up of more than 26,000 individual pieces of steel. The roof is designed to look like a bird's nest, with interlocking pieces that provide shade and protection from the elements.

In addition to its striking design, the stadium is also one of the largest in the world. It can seat up to 91,000 spectators, and it was the site of many memorable moments during the 2008 Olympics, including Usain Bolt's record-breaking 100-meter sprint.

Today, the Bird's Nest is one of Beijing's most popular tourist attractions. Visitors can take a guided tour of the stadium, which includes access to the VIP areas, the changing rooms, and the media centre. There is also a museum located inside the stadium, which features exhibits on the history of the Olympics and the construction of the stadium itself.

In addition to its role as a sporting venue, the Bird's Nest has also become a symbol of modern China and a testament to the country's growing influence on the world stage. Its iconic design has been featured in countless films and television shows, and it has become a symbol of the country's commitment to innovation and progress.

The Bird's Nest is truly a modern architectural wonder, a testament to human creativity and ingenuity. It's unique design and impressive size makes it one of the most impressive structures in the world, and a must-see destination for anyone visiting Beijing. So why not add it to your travel itinerary and experience the awe-inspiring beauty of the Bird's Nest for yourself?

A Spiritual Sanctuary Amidst the City's Bustle

Located in the bustling city of Beijing, the Lama Temple, also known as Yonghe Temple, is a spiritual sanctuary that offers a peaceful respite from the chaos of city life. The temple, which was originally built in the late 17th century as the residence of a prince, was later converted into a Tibetan Buddhist monastery, and today it is one of the most important religious sites in China.

The temple complex is made up of five main halls, each of which houses different artefacts and religious relics. The first hall, known as the Hall of Heavenly Kings, is the largest and most impressive of the five. It features a massive statue of the Maitreya Buddha, as well as intricate carvings and decorations.

The second hall, known as the Hall of Harmony and Peace, is where the monks would meet to discuss important matters. This hall features a statue of the Buddha of the Future, as well as several other important religious figures.

The third hall, known as the Hall of Everlasting Protection, is where the emperor would come to pay his respects to the monks. This hall features a statue of the Sakyamuni Buddha, as well as several other important figures from Buddhist history.

The fourth hall, known as the Hall of the Wheel of Law, is where the monks would study and debate Buddhist philosophy. This hall features several impressive statues, including a large statue of the Manjusri Bodhisattva.

The fifth and final hall, known as the Pavilion of Ten Thousand Happinesses, is where the monks would pray for the well-being of the emperor and the people of China. This hall features a large statue of the Maitreya Buddha, as well as several other important figures.

In addition to its impressive halls and statues, the Lama Temple also features several beautiful gardens and courtyards. These peaceful and serene areas offer a welcome respite from the hustle and bustle of the city, and they provide visitors with a chance to relax and reflect on their spiritual journey.

One of the most unique features of the temple is the massive statue of the Maitreya Buddha, which stands over 18 meters tall and is made entirely out of sandalwood. This statue is considered to be one of the most impressive examples of Buddhist art in the world, and it is a must-see for anyone visiting the temple.

The Lama Temple is also home to a large community of monks, who live and work within the temple complex. These monks are highly respected and revered in Chinese society, and they play an important role in maintaining the spiritual traditions of the temple.

Visitors to the Lama Temple can take a guided tour of the complex, which includes access to all five halls as well as the gardens and courtyards. There are also several souvenir shops located within the temple complex, where visitors can purchase Buddhist artefacts and other spiritual items.

In conclusion, the Lama Temple is a true oasis of peace and serenity in the heart of one of the world's busiest cities. Its impressive halls and beautiful gardens offer a glimpse into the rich spiritual traditions of China, and its community of monks provides a living link to the temple's ancient past. Whether you are a spiritual seeker or simply looking for a break from the chaos of city life, the Lama Temple is a must-see destination for anyone visiting Beijing.

A Tranquil Oasis in the Heart of the City

Beihai Park, located in the centre of Beijing, is one of the city's most beloved landmarks. It is an oasis of tranquillity amid the bustling city, and it offers visitors a unique opportunity to escape the hustle and bustle of modern life and immerse themselves in the beauty and serenity of nature.

The park is a stunning example of traditional Chinese garden design, featuring lush greenery, tranquil ponds, and winding paths that lead visitors through a series of pavilions, temples, and other structures that date back to the Ming and Qing dynasties. One of the park's most iconic features is its White Pagoda, which rises majestically from the centre of the park and offers breathtaking views of the surrounding landscape.

Beihai Park was originally built in the 10th century, during the Liao dynasty, and it has been renovated and expanded several times throughout its long history. The park covers an area of more than 68 hectares, and it is home to a diverse array of flora and fauna, including rare and exotic species that can only be found in China.

Visitors to Beihai Park can spend hours wandering its winding paths and exploring its many attractions, including the Nine-Dragon Wall, a stunning example of traditional Chinese architecture that is adorned with intricate dragon sculptures, and the Five-Dragon Pavilions, a series of ornate pavilions that offer stunning views of the surrounding landscape.

One of the most popular activities in Beihai Park is boating on the lake, which offers visitors a unique perspective on the park's natural beauty and historic architecture. Visitors can rent paddle boats or take a guided tour on a traditional Chinese boat, and enjoy a leisurely tour of the park's many attractions.

Another popular attraction in Beihai Park is the Circular City, a walled structure that was built in the Ming dynasty and served as the imperial palace's outer city during the Qing dynasty. The Circular City is home to many historic structures, including the Nine-Dragon Screen, a magnificent wall that features intricate carvings of dragons.

Visitors to Beihai Park can also enjoy a variety of cultural activities, including traditional Chinese music and dance performances, calligraphy demonstrations, and tea ceremonies. The park is home to several tea houses, where visitors can sample a variety of teas and traditional Chinese snacks while enjoying the park's natural beauty and peaceful atmosphere.

In addition to its many attractions, Beihai Park is also an important cultural site in China, and it has played an important role in the country's history and politics. In the early 20th century, it was the site of several important political rallies, and it was also the site of a famous meeting between Chinese leaders and representatives of the Soviet Union in 1957.

Overall, Beihai Park is a must-see attraction for anyone visiting Beijing. Its stunning natural beauty, rich history, and cultural significance make it one of the city's most unique and beloved landmarks, and it offers visitors a unique opportunity to immerse themselves in the beauty and tranquillity of traditional Chinese culture.

Houhai Lake

Houhai Lake is a popular destination for locals and tourists alike in Beijing. It's a picturesque lake surrounded by traditional Chinese architecture, and it's a hub for nightlife and entertainment.

The lake, which covers an area of over 100 hectares, was once a royal lake during the Yuan, Ming, and Qing dynasties. Today, it's a popular spot for boating and fishing, and there are numerous restaurants, bars, and cafes dotted around its banks.

One of the most popular activities at Houhai Lake is taking a boat ride around the lake. The boats come in a variety of styles, from traditional Chinese dragon boats to modern paddle boats. It's a great way to see the lake and its surroundings and to take in the sights and sounds of Beijing.

The lake is also a popular spot for fishing. Visitors can rent a fishing rod and bait and try their hand at catching some of the lake's many fish. There is a variety of fish in the lake, including carp, catfish, and tilapia.

In addition to boating and fishing, there are plenty of other things to do at Houhai Lake. Visitors can stroll around the lake and take in the beautiful scenery, or they can visit some of the many shops and markets that line the lake's banks.

One of the highlights of Houhai Lake is its nightlife. As the sun sets, the lake comes alive with the sound of music and laughter. There are plenty of bars and restaurants around the lake, and they offer everything from traditional Chinese cuisine to international fare.

One of the most popular areas for nightlife at Houhai Lake is the Drum Tower area. Here, visitors can find a wide variety of bars and clubs, ranging from traditional Chinese bars to modern nightclubs.

But despite the lively nightlife, Houhai Lake still retains a traditional feel. Many of the buildings around the lake are traditional Chinese structures, and there are plenty of traditional Chinese activities to enjoy. Visitors can watch traditional Chinese music and dance performances, or they can try their hand at calligraphy or painting.

For those who want to escape the bustle of the city, Houhai Lake is a tranquil oasis in the heart of Beijing. The lake and its surroundings are beautiful, and there are plenty of opportunities to relax and enjoy the scenery.

In conclusion, Houhai Lake is a must-visit destination for anyone travelling to Beijing. Whether you're interested in boating and fishing, nightlife and entertainment, or traditional Chinese culture, there's something for everyone at Houhai Lake. So pack your bags, and get ready to experience the beauty and excitement of this amazing destination.

A Hub of Contemporary Art and Culture

The 798 Art District is a place where art and culture collide. Located in the Dashanzi area of Beijing, this area was once home to factories that produced military electronics. Today, these factories have been transformed into art galleries, studios, and cafes. The 798 Art District is now a hub of contemporary art and culture, attracting visitors from around the world.

The transformation of the Dashanzi area into the 798 Art District began in the early 2000s. At that time, artists and galleries began moving into the abandoned factories, attracted by the large, open spaces and affordable rent. The district quickly became a hub for contemporary art, with galleries showcasing the works of both Chinese and international artists.

One of the most famous galleries in the 798 Art District is the Ullens Center for Contemporary Art. This gallery was founded by Belgian collectors Guy and Myriam Ullens in 2007 and showcases contemporary art from China and around the world. The Ullens Center also hosts a variety of exhibitions, workshops, and talks throughout the year.

Another must-visit gallery in the 798 Art District is the Pace Gallery. This gallery represents many of the world's leading contemporary artists and has a strong focus on Chinese artists. The Pace Gallery is known for its large, dramatic exhibitions that showcase the works of multiple artists at once.

In addition to galleries, the 798 Art District is also home to some studios where visitors can see artists at work. One such studio is the Red Gate Gallery, which has been in operation since 1991. The Red Gate Gallery represents both established and emerging artists and is known for its support of experimental and avant-garde art.

The 798 Art District is not just a place to see art; it's also a place to experience Chinese culture. The district is home to several cafes, bars, and restaurants that serve traditional Chinese cuisine. Visitors can also find shops selling traditional Chinese crafts and souvenirs.

One of the most unique features of the 798 Art District is its architecture. The buildings in the district were built in the Bauhaus style, a type of modernist architecture that originated in Germany in the early 20th century. The buildings have large windows, clean lines, and a sense of spaciousness that is perfect for displaying contemporary art.

One of the best times to visit the 798 Art District is during the annual Beijing Design Week. This week-long event celebrates the best of Chinese design and includes exhibitions, talks, and workshops throughout the district. During Beijing Design Week, the district is transformed into a creative hub, with designers, artists, and visitors from around the world coming together to celebrate design and innovation.

The 798 Art District is a must-visit destination for anyone interested in contemporary art and culture. With its galleries, studios, cafes, and shops, the district offers a unique glimpse into the world of Chinese art and design. Whether you're an art lover, a designer, or simply someone who appreciates creativity, the 798 Art District is not to be missed.

Chapter 4: Immersing Yourself in Beijing's Culture

Beijing's Opera

Beijing Opera, also known as Peking Opera, is a traditional Chinese art form that originated in the late 18th century during the Qing Dynasty. This unique blend of music, dance, and drama has been enjoyed by audiences across China and around the world for generations. With its rich history and cultural significance, Beijing Opera is truly a window to China's unique and captivating heritage.

At its core, Beijing Opera is a form of storytelling that incorporates a wide range of elements, including music, dance, acrobatics, and elaborate costumes and makeup. The stories told in Beijing Opera are often drawn from traditional Chinese legends, historical events, or classic works of literature. These stories are brought to life through

103

the artful performances of skilled performers, who use a range of techniques and tools to convey emotion and meaning to the audience.

One of the most distinctive features of Beijing Opera is its use of singing, which is used to convey the dialogue and emotions of the characters on stage. The singing in Beijing Opera is highly stylized, with performers using a range of vocal techniques to create a unique and compelling sound. In addition to singing, Beijing Opera also incorporates a range of other musical elements, including percussion instruments, wind instruments, and stringed instruments, which are used to create a rich and complex sound.

Another key element of Beijing Opera is its use of elaborate costumes and makeup, which are used to create highly stylized and symbolic representations of the characters on stage. These costumes are often highly decorative and ornate, featuring intricate patterns, bright colours, and a range of embellishments, including tassels, feathers, and jewellery. Similarly, the makeup used in Beijing Opera is highly stylized, with performers using a range of techniques to create bold, dramatic looks that help to convey the emotions and personalities of the characters they are portraying.

Beijing Opera is also known for its use of acrobatics and martial arts, which are often used to create dynamic and visually stunning performances. Performers in Beijing Opera are highly skilled and trained, using a range of acrobatic techniques to create impressive feats of strength and agility on stage. These performances are often accompanied by music and other elements of the performance, creating a truly immersive and captivating experience for the audience.

In addition to its artistic and cultural significance, Beijing Opera also holds a special place in the hearts of many Chinese people, who see it as a symbol of their country's unique cultural heritage and traditions. Beijing Opera has played an important role in Chinese society for generations, and it continues to be an important part of China's cultural landscape today.

For those who are interested in experiencing the rich and captivating world of Beijing Opera for themselves, there are many opportunities to do so in Beijing and other cities across China. From traditional opera houses to outdoor performances and cultural festivals, there are countless ways to explore and enjoy this fascinating art form. Whether you are a lifelong fan of Beijing Opera or simply looking for a new and unique cultural experience, there is something truly special about this captivating and timeless art form.

Traditional Chinese Medicine

Traditional Chinese Medicine (TCM) is a centuries-old practice that involves the use of herbs, acupuncture, massage, and other techniques to promote health and treat various illnesses. It is a vital part of China's cultural heritage and remains popular to this day, not only in China but around the world.

TCM is based on the belief that the human body is a complex system of interconnected parts and that health depends on maintaining a balance between these parts. When the balance is disrupted, illness can occur. TCM practitioners believe that the body has a natural ability to heal itself and that its role is to support this natural healing process.

One of the key principles of TCM is the concept of qi (pronounced "chee"), which refers to the vital energy that flows through the body. According to

TCM, illness occurs when the flow of qi is disrupted, blocked, or imbalanced. TCM practitioners use a variety of techniques to restore the flow of qi and promote healing.

Herbal medicine is a fundamental part of TCM, and practitioners use a wide range of herbs and other natural substances to treat various conditions. These herbs are often combined into formulas that are tailored to the individual patient's needs. Many of these herbs have been used for centuries and have a proven track record of effectiveness.

Acupuncture is another key component of TCM. This involves the insertion of thin needles into specific points on the body to stimulate the flow of qi and promote healing. Acupuncture is often used to treat pain, but it can also be effective for a wide range of other conditions, including digestive disorders, respiratory problems, and mental health issues.

In addition to herbal medicine and acupuncture, TCM also includes a range of other techniques, including cupping, moxibustion, and massage. Cupping involves the use of suction cups to create a vacuum on the skin, which is believed to promote healing by improving blood flow and stimulating the flow of qi. Moxibustion involves the burning of dried herbs near the skin to stimulate the flow of qi and promote healing. Massage, known as tuina, is used to stimulate the flow of qi and promote relaxation.

While TCM is deeply rooted in China's cultural heritage, it is not limited to Chinese people. In fact, TCM is becoming increasingly popular around the world as people seek out natural, holistic alternatives to Western medicine. Many TCM practitioners now offer their services in countries around the world, and TCM clinics and schools are popping up in many places.

However, it is important to note that TCM is not a substitute for Western medicine, and should not be used as a replacement for medical treatment. Rather, it should be seen as a complementary practice that can be used alongside Western medicine to promote health and well-being.

Traditional Chinese Medicine is a fascinating and powerful practice that has stood the test of time. Its use of natural remedies and techniques to promote healing and balance is both effective and inspiring. While it may not be a cure-all, TCM is a valuable tool in the quest for health and well-being.

Chinese Cuisine

Chinese cuisine is a rich tapestry of flavours, textures, and techniques that have evolved over thousands of years. Beijing, the capital of China, is a hub for some of the most authentic and delicious Chinese cuisine. From crispy Peking duck to savoury dumplings, Beijing has something to offer every food lover.

Peking Duck is undoubtedly the most iconic dish in Beijing, and it's not hard to see why. The dish is made up of roasted duck that has been marinated in a mixture of spices and served with thin pancakes, spring onions, and a sweet bean sauce. The crispy skin and succulent meat are a treat for the taste buds and make for an unforgettable dining experience. Many restaurants in Beijing specialize in Peking Duck, but Quanjude Restaurant is the most famous.

Another popular dish in Beijing is jibing, a type of savoury crepe made with a batter of wheat and mung bean flour, filled with eggs, scallions, and crispy fried dough. This dish is a popular street food in Beijing and can be found on almost every street corner. It's a quick and delicious breakfast option that is loved by locals and visitors alike.

Dumplings, or jiaozi, are a staple of Chinese cuisine, and Beijing has its unique twist on this classic dish. The Beijing-style dumplings are larger and flatter than the traditional dumplings and are filled with pork, chives, and cabbage. They are often served with a dipping sauce made of vinegar, soy sauce, and chilli oil.

Beijing is also famous for its hot pot, a communal meal where diners cook raw ingredients such as meat, vegetables, and seafood in a boiling pot of broth. The hot pot is a fun and interactive dining experience that is perfect for large groups. Hai Di Lao Hot Pot is one of the most popular hot pot restaurants in Beijing and is known for its excellent service and high-quality ingredients.

One of the unique features of Beijing cuisine is its use of offal or organ meats. Offal dishes may not be for everyone, but if you're feeling adventurous, then you should try some of the famous Beijing offal dishes like stinky tofu, braised pig intestines, and barbecued lamb kidney. These dishes are not for the faint of heart, but they are an excellent way to experience the local cuisine.

Beijing is also famous for its street food scene. Wangfujing Snack Street is a bustling pedestrian street that is lined with food stalls selling a variety of snacks and delicacies. From scorpions on sticks to candied hawthorns, there is something to suit every taste.

Beijing cuisine is a delightful combination of traditional and modern flavours that is sure to leave you wanting more. With so many delicious dishes to try, you'll never run out of new culinary experiences to discover. So whether you're a foodie or just looking for some new and exciting dishes to try, Beijing is the perfect destination for a culinary adventure.

Chinese Tea Culture

China is famous for its tea culture, and Beijing is no exception. The city boasts a rich history of tea drinking, with its unique styles and customs. From traditional tea houses to modern tea shops, Beijing offers a diverse range of options for tea enthusiasts to explore and indulge in.

Tea has been an integral part of Chinese culture for centuries. It is believed that tea was first discovered in China during the Tang dynasty (618-907 AD) by the emperor's physician. Since then, tea has been used for its medicinal properties and has become an important part of social and cultural gatherings.

In Beijing, tea drinking has been an essential part of local life for centuries. The city has a long history of tea production and consumption, with many traditional tea houses still operating today. These tea houses offer a glimpse into Beijing's cultural heritage, providing visitors with the opportunity to experience the city's tea culture firsthand.

One of the most famous tea houses in Beijing is the Lao She Teahouse. Located in Qianmen, the heart of Beijing's old city, the Lao She Teahouse was named after the renowned Chinese writer Lao She, who was known for his love of tea. The teahouse offers a variety of teas, including the famous Beijing-style jasmine tea and the traditional black tea from the Yunnan province.

Another popular tea house in Beijing is the Maliandao Tea Street. Located in the southwestern part of the city, the street is home to over 1,000 tea shops, making it the largest tea market in Beijing. Here, visitors can sample a wide range of teas, including green tea, oolong tea, and pu-erh tea, and purchase tea sets and accessories.

Apart from traditional tea houses, Beijing also has many modern tea shops that cater to a younger, more contemporary crowd. One of the most popular of these is the Heytea chain, which specializes in fruit-flavoured teas and has become a sensation among China's younger generation.

For those interested in the history and art of tea, Beijing also has several museums dedicated to tea culture. The China Tea Museum, located in the western suburbs of Beijing, is one such museum. Here, visitors can learn about the history and culture of tea in China and view a wide range of tea-related artefacts, including tea sets, teapots, and tea caddies.

In addition to tea houses and museums, Beijing also has several parks and gardens where visitors can enjoy tea and immerse themselves in the city's tea culture. The Imperial Garden of the Palace Museum, for example, has a beautiful tea house located in the middle of a lotus pond, offering a tranquil setting for visitors to enjoy tea and relax.

In terms of tea varieties, Beijing has a wide range of options to choose from. Some of the most popular teas in Beijing include jasmine tea, green tea, and oolong tea. Beijing-style jasmine tea is a type of scented tea that has a delicate and fragrant aroma, while green tea is known for its fresh and slightly bitter taste. Oolong tea, on the other hand, has a slightly sweet and nutty flavour and is often enjoyed with traditional Beijing-style snacks.

Overall, Beijing's tea culture is a must-see for any tea enthusiast or cultural explorer. Whether you're looking for a traditional tea house experience or a modern twist on tea drinking, Beijing has something for everyone. From sampling different tea varieties to learning about the history and art of tea, a visit to visit Beijing is a chance to immerse yourself in the rich and fascinating world of Chinese tea culture.

Exploring Beijing's Lanes and Alleys on Foot or by Bike

Beijing, a city rich in history and culture, is also known for its unique Hutongs - the traditional narrow alleys and lanes lined with courtyard houses.

These Hutongs are not only a symbol of Beijing's past but also a significant part of the city's present. If you want to experience the true essence of Beijing, a Hutong tour should be on your list of things to do.

There are several ways to explore the Hutongs - on foot, by bicycle, or even by rickshaw. Walking through the narrow alleys is the best way to experience the Hutong's charm, as it allows you to take in the details and observe the daily life of the residents. On a bicycle, you can cover more ground and see more Hutongs in a shorter time, while a rickshaw ride gives you a taste of old Beijing's traditional transportation.

One of the most famous Hutongs in Beijing is Nanluoguxiang. This 800-year-old alleyway is a popular destination for tourists and locals alike, with its unique combination of traditional and modern shops and eateries. You can also find many interesting street vendors selling snacks and souvenirs along the alley.

Another popular Hutong is Dashilar, located in the heart of Beijing's Qianmen area. This Hutong has a rich history dating back to the Ming Dynasty and has undergone numerous transformations throughout the centuries. Today, it is a vibrant commercial area with shops selling traditional Chinese products, such as silk and jade.

For a more immersive experience, you can also join a Hutong homestay program, which allows you to stay with a local family in their traditional courtyard house. This is an excellent opportunity to learn about the daily life and customs of the locals, and to try your hand at making traditional Chinese dishes or practising calligraphy.

During your Hutong tour, you can also visit some of the historical landmarks that are scattered throughout these alleyways. One such landmark is the Drum Tower, located in the heart of the city. This 600-year-old tower was once used to announce the time and alert residents of emergencies.

Another must-see is the Bell Tower, located just north of the Drum Tower. This tower was used to announce the start of the day, and its bell could be heard throughout the city. Today, both towers are popular tourist attractions, and you can climb to the top for a panoramic view of the surrounding Hutongs and the city skyline.

Finally, no Hutong tour would be complete without trying some of the local street food. Beijing's Hutongs are famous for their delicious snacks and delicacies, such as Beijing-style meat skewers, fried dumplings, and traditional desserts. You can also find many trendy cafes and bars hidden in these alleyways, offering a unique fusion of old and new.

In conclusion, a Hutong tour is an excellent way to experience the history and culture of Beijing. Whether you choose to explore on foot, by bicycle, or by rickshaw, you will be transported back in time to the city's rich past. Don't forget to try some of the local street food and visit some of the historical landmarks along the way. A Hutong tour is a unique and unforgettable experience that should not be missed when visiting Beijing.

Chinese Festivals

China is a country rich in traditions and customs, and one of the best ways to experience them is by participating in the many festivals that take place throughout the year. Beijing, being the cultural and political centre of China, is the perfect place to experience some of the country's most vibrant and colourful festivals.

Chinese festivals are deeply rooted in Chinese culture and are a celebration of history, mythology, religion, and tradition. They offer a unique opportunity for locals and tourists to immerse themselves in Chinese culture and gain a deeper understanding of the customs and beliefs of the people.

One of the most important and widely celebrated festivals in China is the Spring Festival or Chinese New Year. It is a time of family reunions, feasting, and exchanging of red envelopes filled with money. The festival usually falls in January or February and is marked by colourful parades, lion and dragon dances, and fireworks displays.

Another festival that is celebrated with great zeal in Beijing is the Lantern Festival. This festival marks the end of the Spring Festival and is celebrated on the fifteenth day of the first lunar month. During the Lantern Festival, the city is decorated with beautiful lanterns, and people gather to watch lantern displays and solve lantern riddles.

The Dragon Boat Festival, which is celebrated on the fifth day of the fifth lunar month, is another popular festival in Beijing. This festival commemorates the death of the famous poet Qu Yuan, who drowned himself in a river to protest against the corrupt government of his time. During the festival, dragon boat races are held on rivers and lakes, and people eat zongzi, a traditional sticky rice dumpling wrapped in bamboo leaves.

The Mid-Autumn Festival, which is celebrated on the fifteenth day of the eighth lunar month, is another important festival in China. It is a time for families to gather and enjoy mooncakes, a traditional Chinese pastry filled with lotus seed paste or red bean paste. The festival is also marked by the lighting of lanterns and admiring the full moon.

Apart from these major festivals, many other festivals and events take place in Beijing throughout the year. The International Dragon Boat Race, Beijing International Music Festival, and the Beijing International Film Festival are just a few examples of the diverse range of events that take place in the city.

Attending a festival in Beijing is not only a great way to experience Chinese culture, but it is also an opportunity to taste traditional Chinese cuisine. During festivals, street vendors sell a wide variety of local delicacies, including jibing, a type of Chinese crepe, and roujiamo, a Chinese-style hamburger.

To fully immerse oneself in the festival experience, it is recommended to dress in traditional Chinese attire. Many tourists choose to rent traditional Chinese outfits, such as qipaos for women and tang suits for men, to fully embrace the festival atmosphere.

Chinese festivals are an essential part of Chinese culture, and participating in them is an excellent way to experience and appreciate the customs and traditions of the country. Beijing, with its rich cultural heritage and diverse range of festivals, is an ideal destination for anyone who wants to experience the vibrant colours, sounds, and tastes of Chinese festivals. So why not plan your trip to Beijing around one of its many festivals and experience the joy of celebrating alongside the locals?

Chapter 5: Practical Information

Chinese Currency and How to Obtain Them

China's currency is the Chinese Yuan Renminbi (CNY) or simply Yuan. When travelling to Beijing, it is important to have an understanding of the currency and how to obtain it. In this article, we will take a look at the Yuan and the various ways you can obtain it in Beijing.

The Yuan is divided into units of jiao and fen. One yuan equals 10 jiao, and one jiao equals 10 fens. However, it is rare to see fen coins and jiao notes as they are not commonly used. The notes are available in denominations of 1, 5, 10, 20, 50, and 100 Yuan.

There are a few ways to obtain Yuan in Beijing:

ATMs:

ATMs are the most convenient and safest way to obtain Yuan in Beijing. You can use your international credit or debit card at most ATMs, which are readily available in the city. However, some foreign cards may not work in certain ATMs, so it's best to check with your bank before your trip. Also, some ATMs may charge a fee for international transactions, so it's important to check with your bank about any fees.

Currency exchange:

Currency exchange is available at most hotels, banks, and airports. However, the exchange rate may not be as good as at the bank, and some currency exchange booths may charge a commission fee. It's important to shop around and compare rates before exchanging currency.

Banks:

You can also exchange currency at most banks in Beijing. It's important to bring your passport with you as it is required for currency exchange. The exchange rate at the bank is usually better than at a currency exchange booth.

Credit cards:

Credit cards are widely accepted in Beijing, especially in large shopping malls and hotels. However, it's important to carry cash as well since some places may not accept credit cards.

When obtaining Yuan in Beijing, it's important to keep in mind a few things:

Counterfeit currency:

Counterfeit currency is a common problem in China, so it's important to be vigilant when accepting notes.

Look for the watermark, the security thread, and the hologram strip to ensure that the note is genuine. It's also a good idea to exchange money at reputable banks and exchange booths.

Bargaining:

Bargaining is a common practice in China, especially in markets and street vendors. It's important to negotiate and haggle for a good price when buying souvenirs or other items.

Tipping:

Tipping is not a common practice in China, and some people may even refuse it. However, in tourist areas, it's becoming more common to tip, especially for tour guides and taxi drivers. It's important to carry small denominations of Yuan for tipping.

In conclusion, the Chinese Yuan is the currency used in Beijing, and there are various ways to obtain it, including ATMs, currency exchanges, banks, and credit cards. When obtaining Yuan, it's important to be aware of counterfeit currency, bargain for a good price, and carry small denominations for tipping. With these tips in mind, you'll be able to enjoy your time in Beijing without worrying about currency exchange.

Accommodation: Best Hotels and Hostels in Beijing

Beijing is a city that offers a wide range of accommodations for every budget, from luxurious hotels to affordable hostels. In this section, we'll explore some of the best options for travellers looking for a comfortable and convenient place to stay in Beijing.

Luxury Hotels

If you're looking for a luxurious and comfortable stay in Beijing, then there are plenty of options to choose from. The city is home to several five-star hotels, many of which offer breathtaking views of the city skyline.

One of the best luxury hotels in Beijing is The Peninsula Beijing. This hotel is located in the heart of the city and offers guests a luxurious experience with its spacious rooms, elegant decor, and world-class amenities. The Peninsula Beijing also has an indoor swimming pool, a spa, and a fitness centre, as well as several dining options serving both Chinese and Western cuisine.

Another great luxury hotel is the Four Seasons Hotel Beijing. This hotel is located in the trendy Chaoyang district and offers guests a luxurious stay with its spacious rooms, elegant decor, and world-class amenities. The Four Seasons Hotel Beijing also has an indoor swimming pool, a spa, and a fitness centre, as well as several dining options serving both Chinese and Western cuisine.

Mid-Range Hotels

If you're looking for a comfortable and affordable stay in Beijing, then there are plenty of mid-range hotels to choose from. These hotels offer comfortable accommodations and great amenities at a reasonable price.

One of the best mid-range hotels in Beijing is the Novotel Beijing Xin Qiao Hotel. This hotel is located in the Dongcheng district and offers guests comfortable rooms, modern amenities, and easy access to some of the city's top attractions. The Novotel Beijing Xin Qiao Hotel also has an indoor swimming pool, a fitness centre, and several dining options serving both Chinese and Western cuisine.

Another great mid-range hotel is the Mercure Beijing Downtown. This hotel is located in the Xicheng district and offers guests comfortable rooms, modern amenities, and easy access to some of the city's top attractions. The Mercure Beijing Downtown also has a fitness centre and several dining options serving both Chinese and Western cuisine.

Hostels

If you're on a budget and looking for affordable accommodations, then there are plenty of hostels in Beijing to choose from. These hostels offer comfortable and clean accommodations at a very reasonable price.

One of the best hostels in Beijing is the Leo Hostel. This hostel is located in the Dongcheng district and offers guests comfortable and clean accommodations at a very reasonable price. The Leo Hostel also has a rooftop terrace, a bar, and a restaurant serving Chinese cuisine.

Another great hostel is the Peking Yard Hostel. This hostel is located in the Xicheng district and offers guests comfortable and clean accommodations at a very reasonable price. The Peking Yard Hostel also has a rooftop terrace, a bar, and a restaurant serving Chinese cuisine.

Overall, Beijing offers a wide range of accommodations to suit every budget and preference. Whether you're looking for a luxurious stay or a budget-friendly option, there are plenty of options to choose from. Just make sure to book your accommodations in advance, especially during the peak travel season.

Eating and Drinking

Beijing is a food lover's paradise, with a vibrant culinary scene that blends traditional Chinese cuisine with contemporary flavours from around the world. From street vendors selling spicy skewers to upscale restaurants serving Peking Duck, Beijing has something to satisfy every palate.

Here's a guide to the best places to eat and drink in Beijing:

Wangfujing Snack Street

Located in the heart of Beijing, Wangfujing Snack Street is a popular destination for locals and tourists alike. The street is lined with food stalls selling everything from scorpion skewers to traditional Beijing snacks like jianbing (a savoury pancake with egg and vegetables) and zhajiangmian (noodles with soybean paste sauce).

Peking Duck

No trip to Beijing is complete without trying Peking Duck, a famous dish that originated in the city. The dish consists of crispy duck skin wrapped in thin pancakes, along with scallions, cucumber, and hoisin sauce. The best place to try Peking Duck is at Quanjude, a restaurant that has been serving the dish since 1864.

Hutong Dumpling Bar

Located in the trendy hutongs (alleys) of Beijing, Hutong Dumpling Bar is a popular spot for those seeking authentic Chinese dumplings. The restaurant offers a variety of dumplings, including pork and chive, shrimp and mushroom, and vegetarian options. The restaurant also offers a cooking class for those who want to learn how to make dumplings themselves.

Jing-A Brewing Taproom

If you're a beer lover, you won't want to miss the Jing-A Brewing Taproom. Located in the trendy Sanlitun neighbourhood, the taproom offers a variety of craft beers, including their flagship Worker's Pale Ale and Flying Fist IPA. The taproom also serves a small menu of bar snacks, including popcorn chicken and spicy edamame.

Da Dong Roast Duck

For a more upscale dining experience, head to Da Dong Roast Duck. The restaurant is known for its innovative take on Peking Duck, which includes a thinner, crisper skin and a lower fat content. The restaurant also offers a variety of other dishes, including seafood and vegetarian options.

Great Leap Brewing

Another popular spot for craft beer enthusiasts, Great Leap Brewing has several locations throughout the city. The brewery offers a variety of beers, including Honey Ma Gold, a honey-infused pale ale, and their Imperial Pumpkin Stout, made with real pumpkin. The brewery also offers a small menu of bar snacks, including cheese plates and charcuterie.

Guijie Street

Located in the Dongcheng district, Guijie Street is a food lover's paradise. The street is lined with restaurants and food stalls selling a variety of Chinese dishes, including spicy Sichuan hotpot, seafood, and barbecued meat. The street is especially lively at night when the neon lights and crowded streets add to the atmosphere.

Beijing offers a diverse and delicious food and drink scene that will satisfy even the most discerning palate. Whether you're in the mood for traditional

Beijing cuisine or contemporary craft beer, there's something for everyone in this vibrant city.

Shopping

Beijing, the capital of China, is a shopping paradise for both locals and tourists alike. From traditional markets selling silk and porcelain to modern shopping malls, the city offers an array of shopping options to suit everyone's tastes and budgets. In this article, we will explore what to buy and where to shop in Beijing.

What to Buy

Silk Products: China is known for its silk production, and Beijing is a great place to buy silk products. You can find everything from silk scarves, ties, and dresses to silk bedding and pillowcases. The best places to buy silk products are the markets in Xiushui and Yashow.

Tea: China is also famous for its tea, and Beijing has some of the best tea shops in the country. You can find a variety of teas, including green tea, black tea, oolong tea, and white tea. The best places to buy tea are Maliandao Tea Street and the China Tea Museum.

Porcelain: Porcelain has been produced in China for centuries, and Beijing is the perfect place to buy porcelain products. You can find everything from vases and bowls to tea sets and figurines. The best places to buy porcelain are Panjiayuan Antique Market and Liulichang Culture Street.

Calligraphy and Paintings: Chinese calligraphy and paintings are renowned for their beauty and intricate designs. You can find a wide variety of calligraphy and paintings in Beijing, ranging from traditional to modern styles. The best places to buy calligraphy and paintings are the National Art Museum of China and the Beijing International Art Palace.

Jade: Jade is a popular gemstone in China, and Beijing is the best place to buy it. You can find everything from jade jewellery to decorative items. The best places to buy jade are Hongqiao Market and Liulichang Culture Street.

Where to Shop

Wangfujing: Wangfujing is one of the most popular shopping streets in Beijing. It offers a range of shopping options, including department stores, shopping malls, and speciality shops. Some of the famous stores in Wangfujing are the Beijing Department Store, the New Dong'an Market, and the Oriental Plaza.

Qianmen Street: Qianmen Street is a historic street that offers a unique shopping experience. It is home to many traditional shops and restaurants that have been operating for centuries. Some of the famous shops on Qianmen Street are Rongbaozhai, Tongrentang Pharmacy, and Quanjude Roast Duck Restaurant.

Xidan: Xidan is another popular shopping area in Beijing. It is home to several large shopping malls, including the Joy City Mall and the Xidan Shopping Center. You can find everything from clothing and electronics to cosmetics and jewellery.

Silk Market: The Silk Market, also known as the Xiushui Market, is a popular destination for tourists looking for affordable souvenirs and clothing. You can find everything from silk products and clothing to electronics and toys. The market is known for its bargaining culture, so be prepared to haggle.

Panjiayuan Antique Market: The Panjiayuan Antique Market is the best place to buy antiques and collectables in Beijing. It is home to over 3,000 stalls selling everything from jade and porcelain to calligraphy and paintings.

Beijing offers a unique shopping experience that combines traditional and modern shopping options. From silk products to calligraphy and paintings, the city has something for everyone. Whether you're looking for luxury brands or affordable souvenirs, Beijing is the perfect destination for a shopping spree.

Chapter 6: Navigating the Beijing Environment

Getting Around

Beijing is a sprawling city, with a population of over 21 million people. It is home to many attractions, ranging from ancient cultural landmarks to modern marvels, and getting around can be a daunting task for many visitors. However, with a bit of knowledge and preparation, navigating the city can be a breeze. This article will provide you with useful information on getting around Beijing via public transportation and taxi services.

Public Transportation

Beijing's public transportation system is extensive and includes buses, subway trains, and taxis. The subway is the most convenient and efficient means of transport in Beijing, with 22 lines covering almost every corner of the city. The subway trains are clean, fast, and affordable, and the stations are well-signposted in both Chinese and English. There are also digital display screens that show the time until the next train arrives.

To use the subway system, you will need to purchase a rechargeable card called a "Yikatong" card. These can be purchased at subway stations and can also be used on buses. You simply tap your card at the turnstile to enter the station and tap it again when you exit. The fare varies depending on the distance travelled, but it is generally between 3 and 9 RMB ($0.50 to USD 1.50). Rush hour on the subway can be crowded, so be prepared to stand.

Buses are another popular mode of public transportation in Beijing. They cover a vast network of routes, and the fares are inexpensive, starting at just 1 RMB (USD 0.15). However, buses can be difficult to navigate for non-Chinese speakers, as the signs and announcements are often only in Chinese. It is helpful to have a map or translator app on your phone to help you figure out which bus to take and where to get off.

Taxis

Taxis are plentiful in Beijing and are a convenient way to travel, especially for short distances or when the subway is not an option. Taxis in Beijing are typically dark green or yellow and have a meter. The flag-down rate is 13 RMB (USD 2) for the first 3 kilometres and then increases in increments based on the distance travelled. There is also a fuel surcharge of 1 RMB (USD 0.15) per trip.

Taxi in Beijing are required to use the meter, and it is illegal for drivers to negotiate fares. However, some drivers may try to negotiate a flat rate, especially if you are travelling a long distance or during rush hour. It is best to insist on using the meter or find another taxi if the driver refuses.

Tips for Getting Around

When travelling around Beijing, there are a few tips to keep in mind to ensure a smooth and hassle-free experience. Here are some of the most important tips:

Avoid rush hour: Beijing's rush hour is from 7:00 am to 9:00 am and from 5:00 pm to 7:00 pm. During these times, the subway can be extremely crowded, and traffic is often gridlocked, making taxis slow and inefficient.

Know your destination in Chinese: If you are travelling to a location where English is not widely spoken, it is helpful to have the address and name of your destination written in Chinese characters. You can show this to the taxi driver or subway attendant to ensure that you are heading in the right direction.

Use a map or translation app: Having a map or translation app on your phone can be a lifesaver when travelling around Beijing. There are many apps available that can help you navigate the subway system, translate Chinese characters, and even hail a taxi.

Be aware of scams: Unfortunately, there are some scams to watch out for when using public transportation or taxis in Beijing.

Safety and Security

Beijing is a fascinating and beautiful city with a rich history and culture, but like any other big city, safety and security are always a concern. Whether you are a local or a tourist, it is important to be aware of the potential risks and take precautions to stay safe and secure. In this article, we will explore some safety and security tips for travelling in Beijing.

Firstly, it is important to be aware of your surroundings at all times, especially when travelling alone or in unfamiliar areas. This means staying alert, avoiding isolated areas and staying in well-lit areas. Avoid displaying expensive items such as jewellery or cameras, and keep your belongings close to you at all times.

When it comes to transportation, the most common way to get around Beijing is by using public transportation such as the subway or buses. These are generally safe, but it is important to keep your belongings close to you and be aware of pickpockets. Be cautious when using taxis, and always use licensed taxis with working meters. If possible, try to use a ride-hailing app like Didi, which is similar to Uber and is generally safer.

When it comes to accommodation, there are many options in Beijing ranging from luxury hotels to budget hostels. When choosing a place to stay, it is important to research the area and read reviews from previous guests. It is also recommended to choose accommodation with good security measures such as security cameras, secure locks, and a safe in your room to store your valuables.

In terms of scams, there are unfortunately some scams that are targeted towards tourists in Beijing. One of the most common scams is the "tea house scam," where friendly locals will invite you to a tea house and then charge exorbitant prices for the tea. To avoid this scam, it is best to decline any invitations from strangers and only go to reputable tea houses or restaurants.

Another common scam is the "art student scam," where a friendly student will approach you and ask to practice their English skills with you. They will then invite you to an art exhibition or shop and pressure you into buying overpriced art pieces. To avoid this scam, it is best to decline any invitations from strangers and only go to reputable art galleries or shops.

It is also important to be aware of the air quality in Beijing, as it can fluctuate depending on the season and weather conditions. During periods of high pollution, it is recommended to wear a mask when outside and limit outdoor activities. You can also check the air quality index online to stay informed and take appropriate precautions.

In terms of emergencies, it is important to know the emergency numbers in Beijing. The emergency number for police is 110, while the number for medical emergencies is 120. If you require help, do not hesitate to call these numbers for assistance.

Overall, Beijing is a safe city with plenty to offer tourists and locals alike. By considering these safety and security tips, you can enjoy your time in Beijing without any worries or concerns. Remember to always stay alert, keep your belongings close to you, and be aware of potential scams and risks.

Language and Communication

If you're planning to visit Beijing, it's important to note that the official language is Mandarin Chinese. While many people in the city may speak English, knowing a few basic phrases in Chinese can go a long way in helping you communicate with locals and make your trip more enjoyable. Here are some useful Chinese phrases and communication tips to keep in mind.

Greetings and Introductions

你好 (nǐ hǎo) - Hello

再见 (zài jiàn) - Goodbye

早上好 (zǎo shàng hǎo) - Good morning

下午好 (xià wǔ hǎo) - Good afternoon

晚上好 (wǎn shàng hǎo) - Good evening

我叫 (wǒ jiào) - My name is...

你叫什么名字？(nǐ jiào shén me míng zì?) - What is your name?

Basic Phrases

8. 谢谢 (xiè xiè) - Thank you

不客气 (bù kè qì) - You're welcome

对不起 (duì bù qǐ) - Sorry

没关系 (méi guān xi) - It's okay

请问 (qǐng wèn) - Excuse me, may I ask...?

Ordering Food

13. 我想点... (wǒ xiǎng diǎn...) - I would like to order...

这个多少钱？(zhè gè duō shǎo qián?) - How much is this?

我不吃... (wǒ bù chī...) - I don't eat...

Transportation

16. 出租车 (chū zū chē) - Taxi

地铁 (dì tiě) - Subway

去...怎么走？(qù...zěn me zǒu?) - How do I get
to...?

Communication Tips

Learn some basic Chinese phrases before your trip.
Even if you don't become fluent, knowing a few key
phrases can help you navigate the city and
communicate with locals.

Download a translation app on your phone. Google
Translate and other apps can be helpful when you
need to translate longer sentences or have a
conversation with someone who doesn't speak
English

Speak slowly and clearly If you're trying to
communicate with someone who doesn't speak

English, try speaking slowly and clearly to help them understand you.

Use gestures and body language. Even if you can't speak the language, using gestures and body language can help you convey your meaning.

Be patient and polite. When communicating with locals, remember to be patient and polite. Even if there is a language barrier, showing respect and kindness can go a long way in making your trip more enjoyable.

Learning some basic Chinese phrases and communication tips, it's also important to be aware of some cultural differences in communication. In China, it is common for people to speak more indirectly and politely than in Western cultures.

It's also important to be aware of cultural differences in body language, such as avoiding direct eye contact or standing too close to someone when speaking

Overall, by taking the time to learn some basic Chinese phrases and communication tips, you can make your trip

Chapter 7: Conclusion

Personal Effects Necessary for the Trip

When planning a trip to Beijing, it's important to pack smart and carry the right items to make your stay comfortable and enjoyable. As a traveller, you need to be prepared for any situation that may arise during your trip, and it starts with the essentials you carry. Here are some personal effects to carry when visiting Beijing.

Passport and Visa: These are the most important documents you need to carry when travelling to Beijing. Your passport should be valid for at least six months and you should have a valid visa to enter the country.

Money: Cash is king in Beijing, and it's always a good idea to carry enough Chinese yuan to cover your expenses. While major credit cards are accepted in some hotels and restaurants, most places prefer cash. You can exchange currency at the airport or in banks and exchange bureaus throughout the city.

Comfortable Walking Shoes: Beijing is a city that requires a lot of walking, so it's important to carry comfortable shoes that can withstand long hours of walking. Flip-flops or high heels may not be the best option, especially if you plan on visiting the Great Wall or other tourist attractions.

Appropriate Clothing: Depending on the time of year you visit, the weather in Beijing can vary greatly. If you visit in the winter, carry warm clothing such as a coat, scarf, and gloves. In the summer, light and breathable clothing is ideal. Be aware of the dress codes for religious sites and temples where modest attire is required.

Sunscreen and Sunglasses: Beijing can be very sunny, especially in the summer, so it's important to protect your skin from the sun's harmful rays. Carry sunscreen with a high SPF and sunglasses to protect your eyes.

Travel Adaptor: China uses a different type of power outlet compared to other countries, so carrying a travel adapter is important if you plan to charge your electronics.

Language Guide: While English is spoken in many tourist areas, not everyone speaks it, and it's always a good idea to carry a language guide or app to help you communicate with locals.

First Aid Kit: Accidents can happen, and it's always good to be prepared. Carry a small first aid kit that includes items such as band-aids, pain relievers, and antiseptic wipes.

Water Bottle: Staying hydrated is important, especially in a city like Beijing where the weather can be hot and dry. Carry a refillable water bottle to stay hydrated throughout the day.

Camera: Finally, don't forget to carry a camera or smartphone to capture the memories of your trip. Beijing is a city with rich history, culture, and stunning sights, and you'll want to capture them all to relive your experience long after you return home.

In conclusion, these personal effects will help you prepare for a comfortable and enjoyable trip to Beijing. It's always important to do some research before travelling to a new destination and to carry the right items that suit your needs. With the right planning and preparation, your trip to Beijing can be a memorable one.

Dos and Don't

When travelling to a foreign country like Beijing, it's important to be mindful of cultural differences and customs. Here are some important Dos and Don'ts to keep in mind during your visit:

DOs:

Learn some basic Chinese phrases: While many people in Beijing speak English, it's always helpful to know some basic Chinese phrases to communicate with locals. This shows respect and appreciation for their culture.

Carry a tissue packet: Public restrooms in Beijing may not always have toilet paper, so it's a good idea to carry a small tissue packet with you.

Dress conservatively: When visiting temples or other religious sites, it's important to dress modestly and respectfully. This means covering your shoulders and knees and avoiding revealing clothing.

Try the local cuisine: Beijing is known for its delicious food, so be sure to try some of the local dishes like Peking duck, jianbing (a type of Chinese crepe), and hotpot.

Take off your shoes when entering someone's home: In many Chinese homes, it's customary to remove your shoes before entering. If you're not sure, ask the host.

Bargain when shopping: Bargaining is a common practice in markets and street vendors in Beijing. However, it's important to be respectful and not haggle too aggressively.

Carry hand sanitiser: Public transportation and crowded areas can be breeding grounds for germs, so carrying hand sanitiser can help keep you healthy.

Respect personal space: In crowded areas, it's important to respect personal space and not push or shove.

DON'Ts:

Don't talk about sensitive topics: Topics such as politics and religion can be sensitive in China, so it's best to avoid discussing them.

Don't give gifts with white wrapping paper: In Chinese culture, white is associated with death and mourning. Giving a gift wrapped in white paper is considered bad luck.

Don't point with your finger: Pointing with your finger is considered impolite in Chinese culture. Instead, use an open hand or nod in the direction you want to indicate.

Don't be loud or rowdy: Loud or rowdy behaviour is considered rude in Chinese culture. Try to keep your voice down in public places.

Don't use chopsticks improperly: Chopsticks are a staple utensil in Chinese cuisine, but using them improperly (such as sticking them straight up in a bowl of rice) is considered impolite.

Don't take photos without permission: It's important to respect people's privacy and ask for permission before taking photos of them.

165

Don't tip: Tipping is not a common practice in China and can be seen as insulting. Instead, it's customary to simply pay the bill.

Don't refuse hospitality: If someone offers you food or a drink, it's considered impolite to refuse. Accepting their hospitality is a sign of respect and appreciation.

In summary, by following these Dos and Don'ts, you can show respect for Beijing's culture and traditions and have a more enjoyable and fulfilling travel experience.

Reflecting on Your Beijing Experience

Travelling to Beijing is an unforgettable experience that leaves a lasting impression on the mind and heart of every traveller. From the rich culture and history to the delectable cuisine, bustling markets, and modern architecture, there is always something to fascinate and inspire visitors. As you reminisce about your Beijing experience, here are some memories, lessons, and inspiration to help you cherish the memories and plan for future trips.

Memories

The memories of your Beijing experience will remain vivid for years to come. You may recall the awe-inspiring sight of the Great Wall of China, the colourful costumes and mesmerizing performances of the Beijing Opera, the bustling hutongs, and the serene beauty of the Summer Palace. Perhaps you also remember the delicious Peking duck, the fragrant tea, and the vibrant nightlife in the city. These memories will forever be etched in your mind, and they will always bring a smile to your face.

Lessons

Travelling to Beijing teaches you valuable lessons that you can apply to your daily life. Firstly, the experience teaches you to appreciate the beauty of different cultures and traditions. It shows you that despite the differences in language, customs, and beliefs, we are all connected by our humanity. Secondly, it teaches you to be adaptable and open-minded. The experience exposes you to new situations and challenges that require you to think on your feet and make quick decisions. Thirdly, it teaches you the importance of communication. As you interact with the locals, you learn the value of effective communication in building relationships and navigating unfamiliar environments.

Inspiration

Your Beijing experience can also inspire you in many ways. It can inspire you to explore more of China's rich history and culture, learn a new language or skill, or take on new challenges in your personal or professional life. The beauty and diversity of Beijing can inspire you to create art, music, or literature that captures the essence of your experience. Moreover, the experience can inspire you to be more conscious of your impact on the environment, support local communities, and seek meaningful connections with people from different backgrounds.

As you reflect on your Beijing experience, you may also want to plan for future trips to the city. Here are some tips to help you make the most of your next trip:

Explore different neighbourhoods: Beijing is a vast city with diverse neighbourhoods that offer unique experiences. Make sure to explore places like Sanlitun, Dashilan, and Nanluoguxiang for a taste of the city's culture and nightlife.

Try different cuisines: Beijing is known for its Peking duck, but there are many other delicacies to try, including hotpot, dumplings, and baozi. Don't be afraid to venture out of your comfort zone and try new dishes.

Learn more about the culture: There are many museums, galleries, and exhibitions in Beijing that offer insights into China's rich cultural heritage. Make sure to visit places like the National Museum of China, the Palace Museum, and the China National Peking Opera Company.

Connect with locals: The locals in Beijing are friendly and welcoming. Engage in conversations, participate in local events, and learn more about their daily lives and experiences.

Travel off the beaten path: Beijing has many hidden gems that are waiting to be discovered. Explore the city's parks, temples, and markets to uncover new experiences.

Reflecting on your Beijing experience can be a source of joy, learning, and inspiration. The memories, lessons, and inspiration that you take away from your trip can enrich your life and shape your perspective in many ways. Whether you plan to return to Beijing or explore other parts of China, always remember to cherish the moments
Planning Your Next Trip: Exploring More of China and Beyond.

If you have already explored the captivating beauty of Beijing, it's time to plan your next adventure in China and beyond. China is a vast country with diverse cultures and traditions, and there's so much to explore beyond the walls of Beijing. From the stunning landscapes to ancient historical sites, to the bustling modern cities, China is a country that never disappoints.

When planning your next trip, there are a few things you need to consider. The first is to determine what type of experience you want to have. Do you want to explore China's natural beauty, experience its rich history and culture, or enjoy its modern cities? Once you have decided, it's time to plan your itinerary and travel arrangements.

One of the most popular destinations in China is the ancient city of Xi'an, which is home to the world-renowned Terracotta Warriors. The city boasts a rich history and culture, and there are plenty of historical sites to explore. You can also visit the nearby Mount Hua and experience the thrill of hiking on its narrow trails, or take a stroll around the charming Muslim Quarter and indulge in its delicious street food.

Another destination worth exploring is the vibrant city of Shanghai. This modern city boasts of towering skyscrapers, high-end shopping centres, and an eclectic mix of culture and entertainment. Take a stroll along the Bund and admire the stunning views of the Huangpu River, or visit the famous Yuyuan Garden and immerse yourself in its traditional Chinese architecture and tranquil atmosphere.

If you want to experience China's natural beauty, head over to the southwestern province of Yunnan. This province boasts of a diverse landscape, ranging from snow-capped mountains to lush forests, and stunning lakes. You can hike along the famous Tiger Leaping Gorge or visit the enchanting Shangri-La and immerse yourself in the local Tibetan culture.

If you're feeling adventurous, consider exploring China's neighbouring countries such as Japan, South Korea, and Vietnam. These countries boast their own unique culture, traditions, and natural beauty, making them the perfect destination for an unforgettable experience.

When planning your itinerary, it's important to consider the logistics of travel, such as flights, transportation, and accommodations. China has an extensive network of high-speed trains that connect major cities, making it easy to travel around the country. There are also plenty of budget-friendly hostels and hotels available, as well as high-end luxury accommodations.

When travelling to foreign countries, it's important to do your research and learn about the local customs, culture, and language. This will not only make your trip more enjoyable, but it will also help you avoid any cultural misunderstandings or unintentional faux pas.

In conclusion, planning your next trip to China and beyond requires careful consideration of your travel goals, itinerary, and logistics. Whether you're looking to explore China's rich history and culture or experience its modern cities and natural beauty, there's something for everyone. By doing your research and planning, you can ensure a memorable and enjoyable trip that will inspire you for years to come.

Printed in Great Britain
by Amazon